Mastering Money

Create the Money You Want, From the Inside Out

Mastering Money

Create the Money You Want, From the Inside Out

Marsha Ferrick, PhD, BCC

Mastering Money

Create the Money You Want, From the Inside Out

Marsha Ferrick, PhD., BCC

Marsha Ferrick, PhD, BCC
Marsha Ferrick Coaching
29805 164th St.
Scottsdale, AZ 85262

www.marshaferrickcoaching.com

To

Melissa

Table of Contents

Why Master Money?

The simple answer to this is that either we master money or money becomes our master. In our culture money often takes on huge proportions in our minds. In some ways that makes sense it is how we barter for our food and shelter. It is on a basic level a need but it does not need to be an all consumed. It does not have to impact our level of happiness but statistically it does make some difference to life satisfaction[1]. Financial independence is having the resources to live a satisfying life, accomplish your dreams and goals, and have more fun doing what you do[2]. So first let's discover what those things are for you.

1. Write in as much detail as you can what your vision of a satisfying life would look like.

---

[1] Robert Wiblin, *Everything you need to know about whether money makes you happy*

[2] Barbara Stanny, *Overcoming, Under Earning*

2. What dreams and goals do you want to accomplish? You may have many but specifically consider the ones you will regret not having done on your death bed. What will be your top three regrets if you do not accomplish them before you die? Be specific.

3. If you had six months to live what would you be doing? Where would you be living? With whom?

4. What would make doing what you do more fun? Be specific.

5. Now reflect on the things that you wrote above. What is it that you want for your life?

   Be specific. How will you know when you have achieved it?

The Journey

When possible it is best to travel this journey with people that will support your journey.

1. Who will you invite to travel with you on this journey to master money?

Mastering money is a journey of change. Change requires an investment of time and money.

This investment in yourself is vital.

2. Are you willing to make this investment in yourself? Why or why not?

3. Are you willing to find the time and the money to make the changes that you need to master money? Why or why not?

Take Ownership

Money is an interesting word. It means many things to many people. Now let's see what money means to you.

1. Complete the following sentence. Repeat the sentence and fill in the blank. When you feel like you cannot go further, write down six more.

    Money is...

2. Now examine what you wrote about money. Consider if each answer characterized money as bad, good, or neutral, just a fact. For example, if you said, Money is evil. You would place that in the bad category. If you said money buys happiness, then place that in the good category. If you said money is green, then place that in the neutral category.

BAD	GOOD	NEUTRAL

3. How do you view money? Have you given money a personification? A life of its' own? Do you believe that money is bad or good? Or do you see it for what it is paper and metal used as an exchange method in our culture? How does your view of money impact how you manage or don't manage your money? How do you allow money to manage you and your life?

4. How would you be different if you did not label money as bad or good? What if you viewed money as simply what it is, a means of barter, paper, and metal?

5. What are the pros and cons of making changes in how you manage your money today?

Pros of Making Changes in Managing $	Cons of Making Changes in Managing $

6. What are the pros and cons of not making changes in how you manage your money today?

Pros of not Making Changes Managing $	Cons of not Making Changes Managing $

7. Where is your comfort zone with money? Consider making the following amounts of money. Close your eyes. How would it feel to have that much money each month in your bank account? What changes would you make? What would you do with it each month? How much would you save it? How much would you spend? How would spend it?

Monthly Earnings	Feelings	Changes	Spending	Saving
$2500				
$5000				
$7500				
$10,000				
$20,000				
$40,000				
$60,000				
100,000				
1,000,000				

8. What did you become aware of as you did the previous exercise? Where was your comfort zone? Where did you become uncomfortable? Did you have a floor or a ceiling? Is there a place where you remain comfortable but to earn more money would make you uncomfortable? Is this uncomfortableness creating a false income ceiling for you?

9. How is your relationship with money a metaphor for other areas in your life? Does it reflect a poor relationship with yourself in which you undervalue your skills? Is it reflective of your intimate relationships? Perhaps you work hard to get and begin a relationship with someone, and at the first sign of stress you throw it all away? Consider all areas of your life and see where themes and patterns emerge that resemble metaphorically your relationship with money.

10. Problems with money are a symptom of other problems in your life. To heal and change your problems with money you must be willing to do both the inner and outer work required. Why or why are you not ready to do the inner and outer work required? What do you need to change in order to change your relationship with money? Do you need to believe you are worthy? Do you need to attend to your issues before you rescue others? Is there a way in which lack of money, poorly managing money, under earning, or over spending keeps in you a familiar state of comfort of discomfort? How do you seek a homeostasis that is comfortable by mismanaging your money?

11. If spending too much or earning too little is your choice, what excuses do you make to abdicate your role in choosing not to do it differently that keep you in financial stress and chaos? Here are some examples.

My boss will never give me a raise.

I have to have this pink purse.

My son is out of money, I have to help him out.

12. Take the excuses from above, and turn them around to empower yourself to make money choices that are good for you. Here are some examples.

My boss will never give me a raise.

- *I have never asked my boss for a raise. She might give me a raise.*

I have to have this pink purse.

- I have 20 purses. I will live without this purse. I certainly do not need this purse.

My son is out of money, I have to help him out.

- I am enabling my son to not manage his money well when I help him out, and setting a poor example for him on how to manage money when I loan him money, and then cannot pay my own bills.

Benefits of Money Mastery

Financial independence has many benefits. Primarily it empowers you by giving you more freedom to choose what you want to do versus what you don't want to do. It produces a less stressful life that allows you to be excited about the present, and the future so you can really live each moment.

1. What are some of the specific benefits you would gain from mastering money, and creating financial independence for yourself?

2. What would you have in your life now that you do not have if you mastered the game of money?

3. What gets in your way of creating the financial independence you want? Be specific.

What separates those that master the game of money from those that don't? It has been noticed that there several things that separate the DIDs and the DID NOTs when it came to creating money[3]. The DIDs made a vow that under earning and over spending where no longer options. They kept that commitment to themselves. They practiced mastery money. They created support for themselves. They learned to put themselves first. They kept meaningful money affirmation where they could see them. They rigorously observed and corrected their actions, and thoughts. They felt the fear and managed their money anyway.

1. Where do you see your strengths, and growing edges in this game of mastering money?

---

[3] Barbara Stanny, *Overcoming, Under Earning* (2005)

Your Story of Money

We have all created stories about money throughout our lives. Here is an opportunity to get clear on what the messages were that we received, and how the help or inhibit us in mastering money in our life today.

1. Write down your memories about money from childhood through adult hood? What were the messages that you created from these memories? What rules did you put in place for yourself about money?

2. How were you given responsibility for money at a young age? Did you earn an allowance? How were you rewarded? What role did money play?

3. What role did gender play in the family when it came to money? Who managed the money? Between your parents? Between your siblings?

4. Did you work while you lived at home? What did you do? What did you learn from these

   experiences, or lack of these experiences?

5. What is the most you have made as an adult? What is the least you have made?

6. What were your parents' experiences with money growing up?

7. What incidents involving money stand out for you? What beliefs have you developed from these incidents?

8. What beliefs do you need to challenge, in order to master the game of money?

Changing Your Beliefs about Money

Changing your beliefs about money is an inside-out game. Mastery starts with our thinking.

Here is a method based on the work of Byron Katie's *The Work* [4] that is helpful for challenging

you the beliefs that you wrote down in the previous exercise.

1. Write down your belief about money. Notice that your belief is a thought.

2. Ask yourself first if your thought statement is true?

   At first consideration, you might say well 'yes that is true, I cannot save money.'

   Yet can you say without any doubt that you cannot save money? My guess is if you are

   reading this book you can save money. You have saved some money for a period of

   time in the past, and you desire to become a better saver than you already are at this

   point in time.

---

[4] Worksheets for Byron Katie's *The Work* can be found at http://thework.com/en/do-work

3. Now exam how you feel when you make that statement to yourself. Write down your observations.

    [   ]

4. Does the thought bring you stress or contentment?

    [   ]

5. What images do you see?

    [   ]

6. What physical sensations arise for you?

    [   ]

7. How do you manage these images and sensations as they present themselves to you? Do you get mad at yourself, or others? Do you become afraid? Angry? Frustrated?

    [   ]

8. How do you treat yourself or others when you have this belief?

9. Who or what would you be or feel without the belief? How would you be different?

10. Now turn the statements arounds in three different ways. Be creative. Find what fits for you. Here is an example.

I can't save money, becomes...

— I save money.

— I look forward to saving money

— I enjoy saving money.

List three ways you could turn your belief around:

11. The next step is to find three examples of when these three new statements were or have been true for you in the past. Using our last example, *I can't save money* becomes:

I save money.

    I saved $5000 when I was in high school to go to college.

    I saved $2000 to buy my wedding dress.

    I save $50 in middle school to buy a bike.

I look forward to saving money.

    I feel safe when I have money in the bank.

    I relax when I have money in the bank.

    When I have money in the bank life is easier.

I enjoy saving money.

    I enjoy the challenge of saving money.

    I love the accomplishment of seeing my money increase each week in the account.

    It is great fun to put off short pluses for longer term gains.

List three ways your statement can be turned around, and give three examples for each one:

12. What new insights are gained from this process of challenging your belief system? How will this assist you in accomplishing the inner mastery of money? Be specific. How can you use thought management technique to take your master of money to the next level? Be specific.

Red Flags

Everyone has their own set of red flags when it comes to money. What are your red flags? When do you know you are in trouble and no longer mastering your money? What things have come up for you past or present that let you know that you need to attend to money matters more diligently?

Growing Edges

Mastering money has many aspects to it. Some you may do very well, yet other areas are overlooked or under managed. For instance, I worked with one couple that couldn't pay their monthly bills yet the wife insisted on giving a gift to every child they knew on their birthdays and holidays. Consider your growing edges. Where do you need to increase your attendance to your money? Savings? Spending? Investments? Gifting? Giving? Cash flow? Over use of credit cards?

To Do

Since we have already established that mastering money is our responsibility, and that we have made the choices that have gotten us to this point, we can now make new choices. Knowing this and given the insights from the previous exercise, what do you need to do differently in order to improve your mastery of money?

For additional titles by Marsha Ferrick, PhD, BCC
visit www.marshaferrickcoaching.com.

For information on coaching contact her at
marshaferrickcoaching@gmail.com.

www.ingramcontent.com/pod-product-compliance
Lightning Source LLC
Chambersburg PA
CBHW081234170526
45165CB00009B/3052